Thank you for reading our Japanese Heritage Songbook. We created the Heritage Songbook Series to promote musical understanding between children, parents, and educators around the world.

We hope you spend many happy hours with the children in your care singing these songs and listening to the accompanying recordings at fiddlefoxmusic.com There, you'll also find coloring pages and other printable activities for all the books in our Heritage Songbook Series.

We've also included color-coded sheet music so young instrumentalists can play and sing along. We recommend using colored rainbow bells that match up with our notation system, but you can also use colored stickers on piano keys or ukulele frets if you would like.

Happy Music-Making!

From the Fiddlefox

www.fiddlefoxmusic.com

4

TABLE OF CONTENTS

JAPANESE HERITAGE
SONGBOOK

Fiddlefox

CHINA

RUSSIA

NORTH
KOREA

SEA OF
JAPAN

SOUTH
KOREA

JAPAN

Tokyo

PACIFIC
OCEAN

PHILIPPINE SEA

1

日本へようこそ
NIHON E YOKOSOU
WELCOME TO JAPAN!

Japan is a nation made of four mountainous islands and many smaller islands. There are sixty active volcanoes and many earthquakes that impact Japan every year. Despite these unpredictable events, Japanese people have thrived on the islands for thousands of years. Japanese culture is deeply connected to the beauty and harmony of nature.

Japanese children are expected to work hard and put the needs of their families, teachers, and communities first.

Today, Japan creates some of the world' most popular electronics, pioneering in the fields of entertainment, technology, and robotics.

さくら さくら
SAKURA, SAKURA

さくら さくら やよいの空は
SAKURA, SAKURA, YAYOI NO SORA WA
SAKURA, SAKURA, CHERRY BLOSSOMS COLOR THE SKY

9

みわたす かぎり かすみ か くもか
MIWATASU KAGIRI KASUMI KA KUMO KA
PINK-WHITE SNOW HOW QUICKLY YOU FLY,
LIKE A CLOUD THAT'S PASSING ME BY

10

におい ぞ いずる
NIOI ZO IZURU
Sweet Aroma, sweeter to spy

11

いざや いざや みに ゆかん
IZAYA, IZAYA, MI NI YUKAN
COME ON OUT! COME ON OUT! COME AND FEAST YOUR EYE!

Sakura, sakura

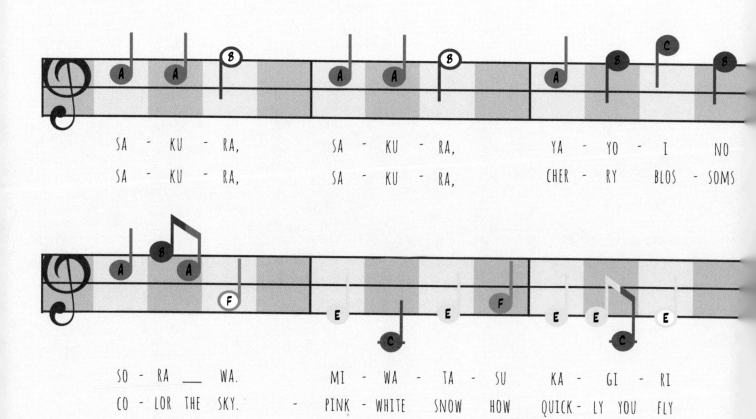

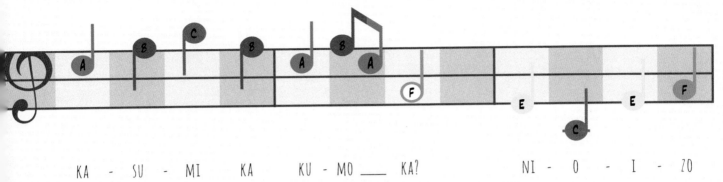

KA - SU - MI KA KU - MO ___ KA?
LIKE A CLOUD THAT'S YANG PAS - SING ME BY.

NI - O - I - ZO
SWEET A - RO - MA,

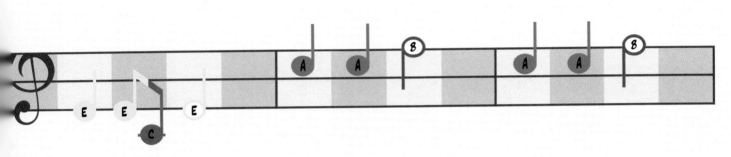

I - ZU - RU.
SWEET - ER TO SPY.

I - ZA - YA,
COME ON OUT!

I - ZA - YA
COME ON OUT!

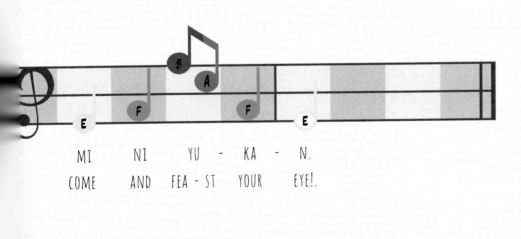

MI NI YU - KA - N.
COME AND FEA - ST YOUR EYE!.

ぞうさん
ZOU-SAN
ELEPHANT

ぞうさん ぞうさん
ZOU-SAN ZOU-SAN
"ELEPHANT, ELEPHANT

15

おはな が ながい の ね
OHANA GA NAGAI NO NE
HOW'D YOU GET YOUR TRUNK TO BE SO LONG?"

16

そうよ、かあさんも
SOU YO, KAASAN MO
"HONESTLY, DON'T ASK ME . . .

ながい のよ!
NAGAI NO YO!
I GET IT FROM MY MOM!"

18

Zou-san
Elephant

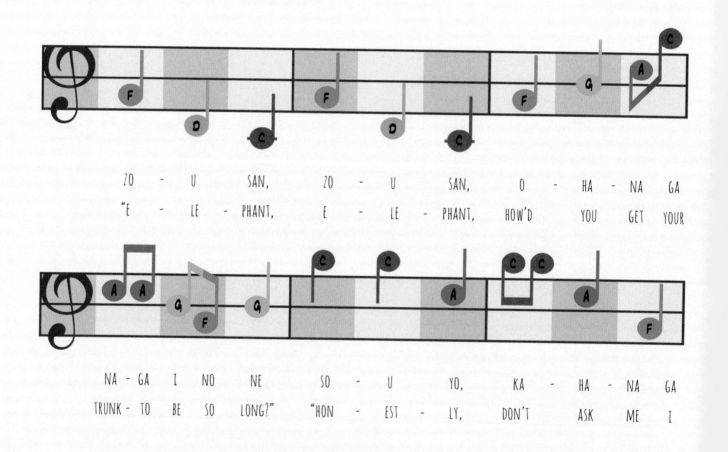

ZO - U   SAN,   ZO - U   SAN,   O - HA - NA   GA
"E - LE - PHANT,   E - LE - PHANT,   HOW'D   YOU   GET   YOUR

NA - GA   I   NO   NE   SO - U   YO,   KA - HA - NA   GA
TRUNK - TO   BE   SO   LONG?"   "HON - EST - LY,   DON'T   ASK   ME   I

どんぐり ころころ
DONGURI KOROKORO
ACORN IS ROLLING, ROLLING

どんぐり ころころ どんぶりこ
DONGURI KOROKORO DONBURIKO
ACORN IS ROLLING, ROLLING: ACORN IS GONE

21

お池に はまって さあ 大変
OIKENI HAMATTE SAA KAIHEN
FELL FROM THE TREE TOPS AND DOWN INTO THE POND

22

どじょう が 出て来て 今日は
Dojou ga detekite konnichiwa
Loaches are singing, singing: They say "hello"

23

坊ちゃん 一緒に 遊びましょう
BOTCHAN ISHO NI ASOBIMASHOU!
COME AND PLAY WITH THE FISHES DOWN BELOW!

NOTES USED

C D E F G A B C

DONGURI KOROKORO
ACORN IS ROLLING, ROLLING

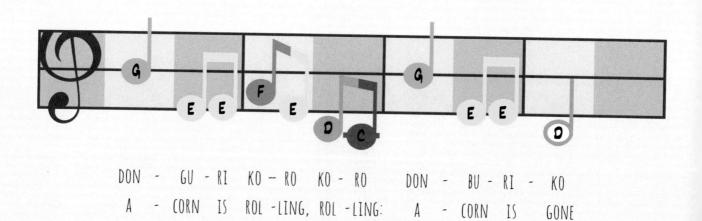

DON - GU - RI KO - RO KO - RO   DON - BU - RI - KO
A - CORN IS ROL -LING, ROL -LING: A - CORN IS GONE

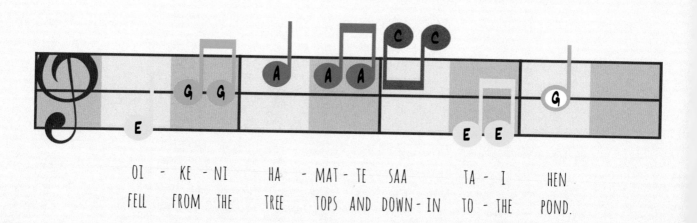

OI - KE - NI   HA - MAT - TE SAA   TA - I   HEN
FELL FROM THE   TREE TOPS AND DOWN - IN TO - THE POND.

25

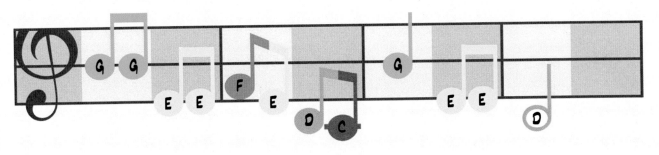

DO - JO -U GA DE - TE - KI - TE   KON - NI - CHI - WA
LOA   -   CHES ARE SING - ING, SING - ING: THEY - SAY "HEL - LO!

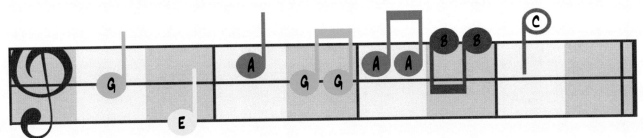

BOC   -   CHAN   IS - SHO NI A - SO - BI - MA - SHOU.
COME   AND   PLAY WITH THE FISH - ES DOWN BE - LOW!"

雪 や こんこ
YUKI YA KONKO
SNOWFLAKES ARE FALLING

雪 や こんこ 霰 や こんこ
YUKI YA KONKO, ARARE YA KONKO
SNOWFLAKES ARE FALLING, HAILSTONES ARE FALLING

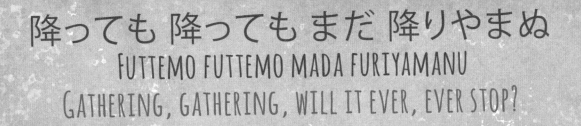

降っても 降っても まだ 降りやまぬ
FUTTEMO FUTTEMO MADA FURIYAMANU
GATHERING, GATHERING, WILL IT EVER, EVER STOP?

犬 は 喜び 庭 駈けまわり

Inu wa yorokobi, niwa kakemawari

My puppy dog is very happy jumping in the garden

29

猫 は 火燵 で 丸くなる
NEKO WA KOTATSU DE MARUKUNARU
INSIDE THE HEATER'S ON WITH MY CAT ON TOP

YUKI YA KONKO
SNOWFLAKES ARE FALLING

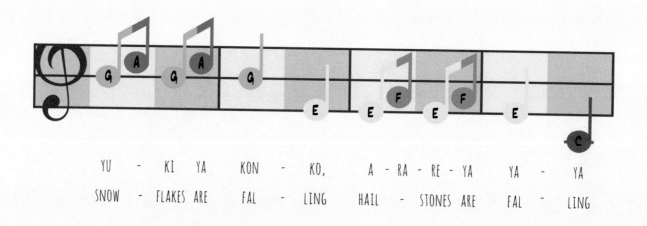

YU – KI YA KON – KO, A - RA - RE - YA YA – YA
SNOW – FLAKES ARE FAL – LING HAIL – STONES ARE FAL – LING

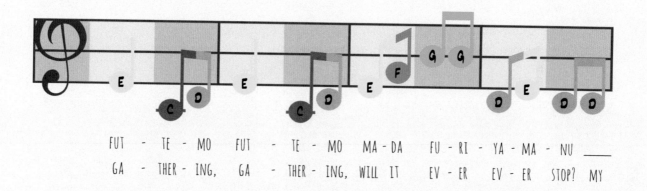

FUT – TE – MO FUT – TE – MO MA-DA FU-RI-YA-MA-NU ___
GA – THER-ING, GA – THER-ING, WILL IT EV-ER EV-ER STOP? MY

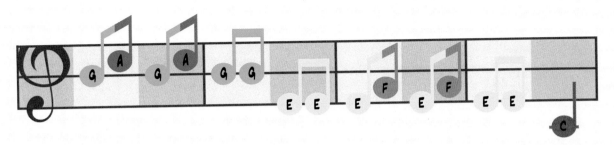

I - NU WA YO - RO - KO - BI NI - WA KA - KE - MA - WA - RI,
PUP - PY DOG IS VE - RY HAP - PY JUMP - ING IN THE GAR - DEN

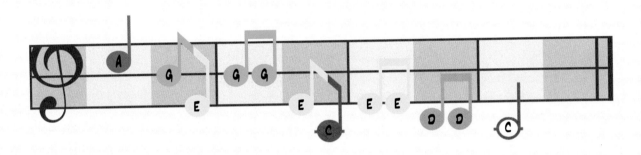

NE - KO WA KO - TA TSU DE MA - RU KU - NA - RU.
IN - SIDE MY HEAT - ER'S ON___ WITH MY CAT ON TOP.

BRING A WORLD OF MUSIC HOME WITH
FIDDLEFOX WORLD HERITAGE SONGBOOKS!

Available on iBooks, Kindle and Spotify!
www.fiddlefoxmusic.com